Mammals Who MORPH

Book Three

WITHDRAWN

The Universe Tells Our Evolution Story

By Jennifer Morgan

Illustrated by Dana Lynne Andersen

Dawn Publications

Dedications

To my grandmother, Barbara Morgan, who told me stories of dancing atoms, and to my son, Morgan Martindell, whose questions evoked these stories into being. — JM

I dedicate this book to the Living Spark of Eternity enshrined within each atom of creation, may Thy radiance be revealed; and to the community of souls ever expanding within life's spiraling evolution, may we awaken to the glory that shines from within. — DLA

Acknowledgments

Sister Miriam MacGillis (Genesis Farm, Blairstown, NJ), Larry and Jean Edwards, Brian Swimme and Thomas Berry continued to be my polestars. Classes and discussions with Princeton University professors Dr. Alan Mann, Dr. Janet Monge, Dr. Jean Altmann, and Dr. Rena Lederman, were fascinating and foundational. Mark Henry, retired microbiologist, was my hero of all heroes . . . always there, ready to take panic phone calls, do research, and check punctuation. My Epic of Evolution Group – Mary Coelho, Susan Curry, Ralph Copleman, Paul Morgan, Maria Myer, Andy Smith, Bob Wallis and Katherine Balthazar – were my toughest critics. Girls in the class of 2010, Stuart Country Day School, Princeton, NJ gave lots of ideas. Dr. Connie Barlow and Michael Dowd helped with insights and twists of phrase. Dana Lichstrahl, Merrill Hemond, Linda Fitch, Gail Worcelo, Bernadette Bostwick, Tara Quigley, Betsy Rizza, Herb Simmens, Karen Chaffee, Aline Johnson, Bill Sloane, Brian Tucker, and the Mullen family helped lighten and smooth the story. Glenn Hovemann and Muffy Weaver, owners of Dawn Publications, turned visions into reality. To Dana Lynne Andersen, I say . . . "Wow, we did it!" Seven-year-old Conrad Kosowsky gave his opinions. The extended Morgan clan, particularly Lucas (age 7) and Theo (age 4) Curran gave pivotal suggestions. My son, Morgan Martindell, grew into a strapping 6'3", 15 year old basketball player. Thanks Morg for always telling me the truth, as in "Mom, that part really sucks," and giving great suggestions. Thomas Berry says that Great Work brings together great fellow travelers. How right he is! Blessings!

Library of Congress Cataloging-in-Publication Data

Morgan, Jennifer, 1955-
  Mammals who morph : the universe tells our evolution story : book 3 / by
Jennifer Morgan ; illustrated by Dana Lynne Andersen.-- 1st ed.
    p. cm. -- (A sharing nature with children book)
  ISBN 1-58469-084-4 (hardback) -- ISBN 1-58469-085-2 (pbk.)
  1. Evolution (Biology)--Juvenile literature. I. Andersen, Dana Lynne,
ill. II. Title. III. Series.

QH367.1M67 2006
569--dc22

2005035807

Printed in China
10 9 8 7 6 5 4 3 2 1
First Edition

Design and computer production by Patty Arnold, Menagerie Design and Publishing

Dawn Publications
12402 Bitney Springs Road
Nevada City, CA 95959
530-274-7775
nature@dawnpub.com

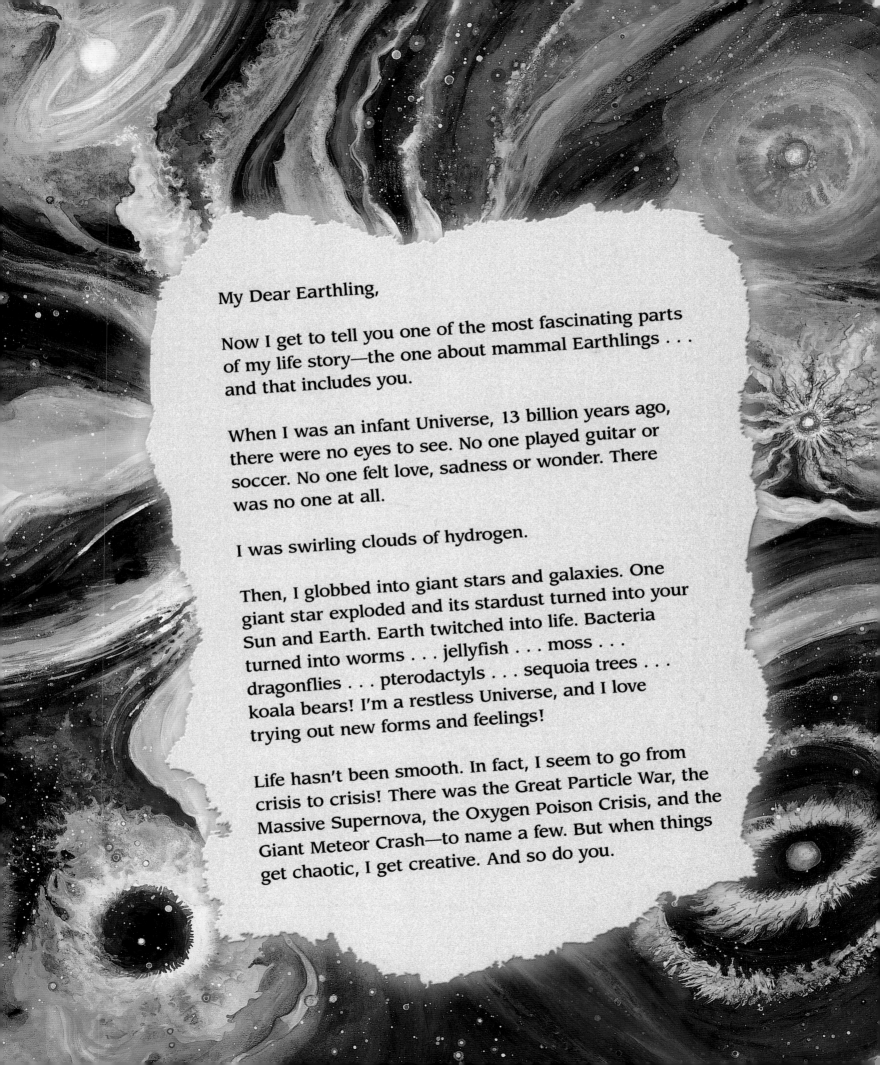

My Dear Earthling,

Now I get to tell you one of the most fascinating parts of my life story—the one about mammal Earthlings . . . and that includes you.

When I was an infant Universe, 13 billion years ago, there were no eyes to see. No one played guitar or soccer. No one felt love, sadness or wonder. There was no one at all.

I was swirling clouds of hydrogen.

Then, I globbed into giant stars and galaxies. One giant star exploded and its stardust turned into your Sun and Earth. Earth twitched into life. Bacteria turned into worms . . . jellyfish . . . moss . . . dragonflies . . . pterodactyls . . . sequoia trees . . . koala bears! I'm a restless Universe, and I love trying out new forms and feelings!

Life hasn't been smooth. In fact, I seem to go from crisis to crisis! There was the Great Particle War, the Massive Supernova, the Oxygen Poison Crisis, and the Giant Meteor Crash—to name a few. But when things get chaotic, I get creative. And so do you.

Your Earth is one of my most creative planets. Over the last 65 million years, Earth dreamed up all kinds of mammal Earthlings . . .

* rabbit-sized camels,

* elephants with teeth on the tips of their trunks,

* armored glyptodonts (GLIP-tuh-donts) who whack each other with spiked tails,

* baby bats who cling to their mothers as they fly,

* whales who sing love songs,

* giant sloths who sleep all day,

* and humans who gape at stars and ask, "Where did we come from? Why are we here?"

How did Earth's mammal dreams come true . . . and how did you become *you*?

To tell the story, we have to go way back, before there were humans, or even horses or camels or squirrels. Once upon a time, long, long ago . . .

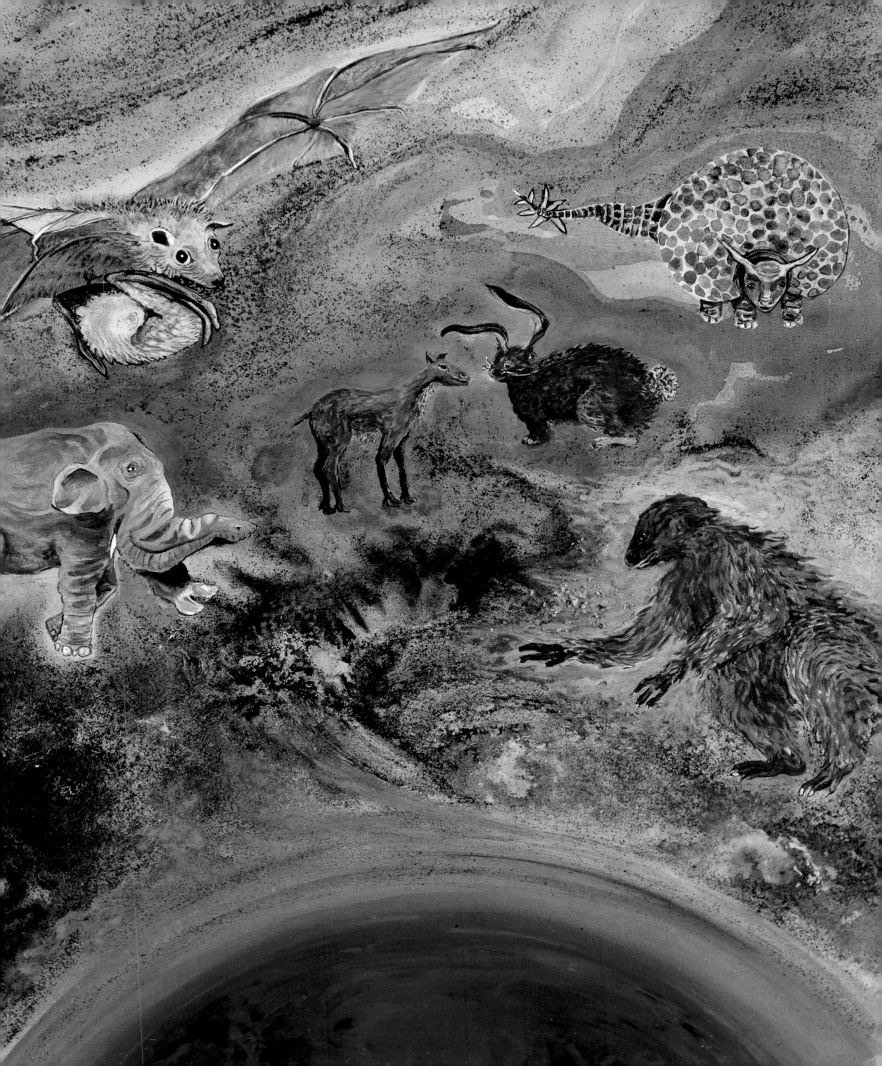

Giant dinosaurs roamed everywhere and mousy mini-mammals lived in trees. Most were so tiny that one could take a nap in the palm of your hand. They slept during the day, and scurried around at night.

Dinosaurs ruled the days, but mini-mammals ruled the nights.

Where did those mini-mammals come from? They evolved out of reptiles when their scales turned into hair. Unlike their reptile ancestors, most mammals didn't lay eggs. Instead, mothers carried their growing babies inside themselves for awhile, and then gave birth. But the little bare-skinned newborns with scrunched up eyes couldn't live on their own. So, mammal moms began making the most amazing stuff—milk.

When the Great Meteor hit, 65 million years ago, Earth roared with earthquakes and fire, then went dark and very cold. Every single dinosaur died.

Look around today as hard as you can. Down the street, under your bed, you won't find dinosaurs anywhere. If you look up into trees, though, you *will* find descendents of dinosaurs who survived the horrible disaster, because they had already morphed into a new kind of Earthling—birds.

But your ancestors, the mammals, scraped by on cockroaches and frozen dinosaur dinners.

Science concepts: Out of reptiles . . . mammals and dinosaurs; Mammals, milk and mother love (see page 41) **7**

Earth wasted no time filling in the empty spaces left by the dinosaurs. Morphing mini-mammals were on the move. The more they moved, the more they morphed; the more they morphed, the more they moved.

**Little by little, land, sea and air
began to shape the mammals to come —**

**Trees sculpting hands
for grasping branches.
Land molding paws and hooves.
Water forming fins.
Air shaping wings.**

It took millions and millions of years. What would these moving, morphing mammals turn into? I wasn't sure. One thing I did know . . . this was an incredible adventure.

Fifty million years ago, steamy hot rainforests stretched from pole to pole.

Plants turned sunlight into huge amounts of roots, shoots, leaves, flowers, fruits and seeds. One mammal you know—the horse—already trotted about and nibbled fruit in the rainforest. But you wouldn't recognize it. It was about the size of a cat, and had cat-like padded feet.

Giant Gastornis birds could catch and snatch up horses with huge bone-crushing beaks.

Yes, birds ate horses back then.

But the giant birds had predators too. Thousands of army ants could overwhelm a Gastornis and bite its body into tiny pieces. And army ants had *their* predators— little mammals with long floppy noses who slurped tasty ants, and chewed them to a nice mash.

There was so much feasting going on . . . plants eating sunlight, animals eating plants and each other.

That's how energy flowed from the sun . . . and was transformed into Earthlings everywhere.

Science concepts: Earth has a temperature; Flowering plants, birds spread; The energy feast. (see page 41) *11*

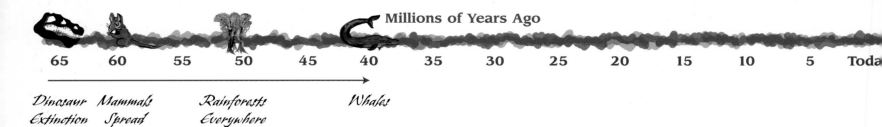

Around the same time, hippopotamus-like mammals appeared. Some day, their ancestors would be true hippos. Others would turn into very different kinds of mammals. It all started on the edge of the sea.

One hot day . . .
some hippo ancestors wanted to cool off.
They started swimming in the ocean.
Whew! What a relief!

There were lots of fish to eat and water supported their bulky bodies. Life was so much easier in the water. Why go back to land? They moved deeper into the sea. Over generations, their nostrils moved to the tops of their heads and turned into blowholes—so much better for breathing while swimming. Gradually their front legs morphed into fins. Their tails morphed into powerful flukes. For a long time, funny little back legs hung on, then finally disappeared. They learned to leap high out of the water and called to each other with songs that rumbled through the sea. Some grew bigger than dinosaurs, but they were still mammals, nursing their babies deep under water.

What mammals chose
to return to the sea,
where all life once began?
Whales and dolphins!

Millions of Years Ago

| 65 | 60 | 55 | 50 | 45 | 40 | 35 | 30 | 25 | 20 | 15 | 10 | 5 | Today |

Dinosaur
Extinction

Mammals
Spread

Rainforests
Everywhere

Whales

Rainforests
Shrink

Grass
Spreads

Earth itself was morphing too.

Massive moving chunks of Earth's crust floated on top of molten rock deep underground. When chunks crashed slow-motion into each other, mountains grew. The Himalayas, Earth's highest mountains, rose up when India crunched into Asia. Until now, Earth had been covered with warm tropical rainforests. But then, mountain winds began to blow. Cold ocean currents began to flow. Rainforests shrank and plains appeared. Ice spread across the poles. Brrrrr!

As Earth cooled, a little plant began to spread and would change things forever. You know it well—grass!

Horses moved into wide-open plains where they ate grass and fertilized it. As grass and horses fed one another, they also shaped each other. Unlike other plants, grass grew from the bottom so it didn't get damaged when the top was eaten. In fact, it got stronger and denser, just as a lawn grows better when cut! Over a long time, horses changed too. Once they were tiny, had padded feet, ate fruit and lived in the jungle. Then they grew big, had just the right teeth for grinding grass, and galloped across plains on hard hooves.

Horses loved grass and grass loved horses. Do you see how everything evolves together?

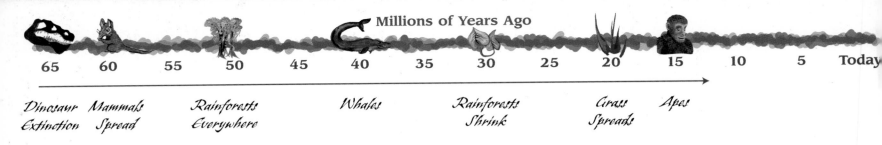

Millions of Years Ago

65   60   55   50   45   40   35   30   25   20   15   10   5   Today

Dinosaur *Mammals*   *Rainforests*   *Whales*   *Rainforests*   *Grass*   *Apes*
Extinction *Spread*   *Everywhere*   *Shrink*   *Spreads*

I've already told you ninety-nine percent of my life story! And still, there are no humans. But there are primates in trees, like lemurs and monkeys, the ones with grasping fingers and eyes that look straight ahead. Over a long time, monkeys evolved into another kind of primate—apes without tails.

Your direct ancestors were primates living in forests near grasslands. I'm talking about Africa's awesome apes.

Super-curious and playful, those apes loved the social life—eating in groups and watching who does what with whom. They expressed their feelings of happiness, anger, and love through chattering, throwing tantrums, and grooming. They cared deeply for each other. And when one died, the others mourned.

They were cooperative and very cultured.

Apes learned their group culture from their elders. In one ape group, young daughters and sons learned from their moms how to crack nuts with a rock, sometimes whacking their thumbs at first. Ouch! In a different forest, another group never cracked nuts; they learned how to stick twigs into termite holes and pick off the tasty termites with their lips.

Wow! Apes were using tools!

Apes can hug and comfort each other tenderly. But sometimes it's a very different story, especially with strangers.

One day, the males in an ape group were conducting their weekly patrol, walking single file around the boundary of their territory. Then, snap! A branch broke nearby. A neighboring male had strolled into their territory by accident. Males in the defending group hollered excitedly to each other. Their alarm calls pierced the forest. Like commandos on a mission, they signaled to one another, divided up, surrounded the stranger and at the end of a brutal gang attack, the stranger lay dead.

The defending group communicated very well with each other. They were a team. But why didn't they communicate with the stranger? Why didn't they give the stranger, who meant no harm, a chance to flee? They could have befriended the stranger. They might have allowed him to stay for a while, then go back to his own territory. But they didn't.

Though incredibly smart, primates couldn't choose between lots of different ways to behave toward strangers. Not yet!

Science concepts: Cooperation within (and competition between) groups (see page 42) *19*

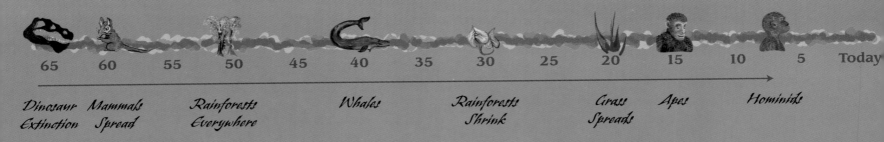

My adventure was about to speed up and become more dramatic than ever before. It started with small changes—a hip adjustment here, straighter and stronger knees there.

In Africa, some of Earth's awesome apes stopped walking on all fours. They stood upright. Wow! They could use their hands even more!

Hands could grasp and carry, fold and throw, twist and poke, carve and stroke. With nimble fingers and sharpening minds, they could make stone tools . . . build castles . . . dunk basketballs and play the violin! Whoa! I'm getting way ahead of myself. Let's get back to the story.

Two-legged, two-handed Earthlings began roaming the Earth.

Lots of different groups of hairy ape-like Earthlings started popping up all over. They were about four feet tall, and had large jaws and teeth. They dined on gooey grubs and worms, leaves, nuts, berries and monkey brains. Yum!

Once, I was swirling clouds of hydrogen. Over billions of years, I turned into birds, horses, grass, whales. And now . . . I was hominids too. Yes, I was becoming human.

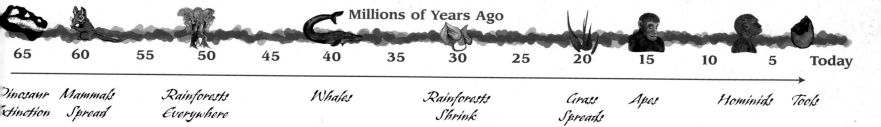

One kind of hominid had a high-powered brain that needed lots of energy . . . so they had to eat and eat and eat.

But back then, the best hunters around weren't human. They were fierce carnivores, especially those dog-like hyenas and huge saber-toothed cats. They sometimes ate humans for lunch. Oh yes, dear Earthlings, your early human ancestors were more often the hunted than the hunter. Then things started to change. Humans in packs—signaling to each other and armed with sticks and stones—learned how to steal meat from those fierce dogs and cats. After chowing down on raw meat, these hungry humans sliced into bones with stone tools and scraped out the fatty marrow—a great food for growing bold and brilliant brains! Who were these humans? *Homo habilis*, the "Handy Man."

Then a tall and slim kind of human, *Homo erectus*, the "Upright Man," showed up on the African grassland, living alongside *Homo habilis*. They, too, followed dogs and cats in search of meat and marrow.

Homo erectus fanned out across the continent. Some walked out of Africa and far beyond. *Homo habilis* vanished.

Science concepts: Dogs and cats: from human foe to friend (see page 42)
23

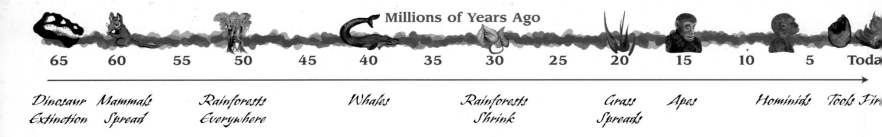

Millions of Years Ago

| 65 | 60 | 55 | 50 | 45 | 40 | 35 | 30 | 25 | 20 | 15 | 10 | 5 | Toda |

Dinosaur Extinction Mammals Spread Rainforests Everywhere Whales Rainforests Shrink Grass Spreads Apes Hominids Tools Fire

Imagine a group of traveling *Homo erectus* families. They're hungry, cold and huddled in a small dark cave during a thunderstorm. CRACK! A lightning bolt strikes a nearby tree and sets it on fire.

They're terrified. But one brave person approaches the fire, grabs a blazing stick and brings it back to the group. No Earthling had ever done that before. Shrieks fill the cave as several humans scramble away in fear. Then they realize that this small fire won't hurt them—as long as they don't touch it. Ah, the warmth feels so good . . . and they can see by its light, even though night is falling. One of them feeds the fire another stick.

Wow! Humans tamed FIRE!

For thousands of years, humans clustered around fires . . . grunting, poking and pointing to communicate with each other. They didn't have words. Not yet! They looked up at the moon and stars. They listened to dogs howling in the distance.

More and more, they awakened to a world of wonder all around them.

Millions of Years Ago

| 65 | 60 | 55 | 50 | 45 | 40 | 35 | 30 | 25 | 20 | 15 | 10 | 5 | Today |

Dinosaur Mammals   Rainforests   Whales   Rainforests   Grass   Apes   Hominids Tools Fire
Extinction Spread   Everywhere   Shrink   Spreads

Thousands of years later came the great hunters, *Homo neanderthalensis*, the Neanderthals. One day, a group of males crouched in tall grass. They were muscular with strong bones, and their foreheads jutted out above their eyes. They followed a pack of dogs that had found a herd of mammoths. Scared, but hungry and determined, they hid. Then . . .

They jumped up and killed a mammoth with spears.

Around a crackling fire that night, men, women, children and dogs devoured roasted hunks of mammoth and roots gathered by the women. Dogs and humans were becoming friends. With shouts, grunts and simple words, the humans excitedly shared stories about the great hunt.

Yes, humans were beginning to speak!

Of course, communication between Earthlings was nothing new. Bacteria had been sending chemical messages for billions of years. Bees had been dancing their messages. Whales sang to each other. Apes grunted and shouted. But the awesome thing about words is that they can be combined in lots of different ways.

The more they talked, the more they thought. The more they thought, the more they talked.

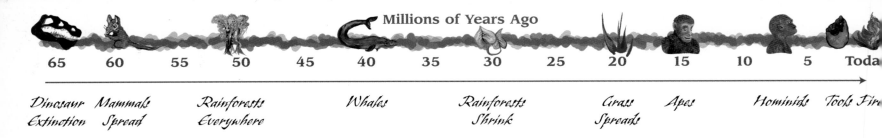

Millions of Years Ago

65   60   55   50   45   40   35   30   25   20   15   10   5   Toda

Dinosaur   Mammals   Rainforests   Whales   Rainforests   Grass   Apes   Hominids   Tools Fire
Extinction Spread   Everywhere   Shrink   Spreads

Humans mixed and morphed and turned into another kind of human, one with a powerful imagination.

They had high foreheads and their bones were more delicate than other humans. With artistic fingers and minds, they made jewelry and, about 30,000 years ago, painted horses on cave walls.

Who were they? *Homo sapiens*, the humans—like you—who live today.

All the other kinds of humans, even the Neanderthals, vanished. Now *Homo sapiens* were Earth's only humans. They descended from generations and generations of humans who lived before them.

They hiked through Africa, Europe and Asia. When a bridge of ice connected Asia to Alaska, a small band slid their way into North America. What were they thinking? They had no maps. Did the polar bears show them where to go?

Wherever they went, *Homo sapiens* delighted in clouds, flowers and rain. They beat drums, played melodies on bone flutes, danced, laughed, and cried. They asked questions like, "What holds up the moon? What are those lights in the night sky? Where did everything come from?" Somehow, they knew that the Universe had a beginning.

Across the planet, they told stories about how I, the Universe, was born.

Millions of Years Ago

| 65 | 60 | 55 | 50 | 45 | 40 | 35 | 30 | 25 | 20 | 15 | 10 | 5 | Today |

Dinosaur Extinction · Mammals Spread · Rainforests Everywhere · Whales · Rainforests Shrink · Grass Spreads · Apes · Hominids · Tools · Fire

There were no more saber-toothed cats, and most dogs were now friends with humans. Humans didn't have many predators any more, so they multiplied. Over time, there were so many humans that it was hard to hunt enough game and find enough roots and fruit for everyone. Then, a strange thing happened.

On every continent, about 10,000 years ago, humans noticed that plants make seeds . . . that sprout into . . . more plants.

Humans began to grow their own fruits and vegetables. They grew grains too—wheat, rice and corn. Grains are members of the grass family. Remember how horses loved grass? Now humans formed a partnership with grass too!

Humans started making things out of food they grew. They ground wheat, added water, and baked it into bread. They ground cocoa seeds, added water, and stirred up hot chocolate. Delicious!

They saw how life came out of the Earth and grew with sunlight. What a great mystery! They thanked Sun and Earth.

Science concepts: Agriculture (see page 43) **31**

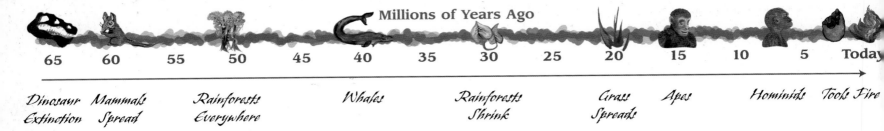

Millions of Years Ago

65   60   55   50   45   40   35   30   25   20   15   10   5   Today

Dinosaur   Mammals   Rainforests   Whales   Rainforests   Grass   Apes   Hominids Tools Fire
Extinction Spread   Everywhere   Shrink   Spreads

Humans became partners with lots of other Earthlings.

Humans gave food; goats gave milk, sheep gave wool, and horses carried humans around. Humans clumped into villages where they traded with each other—milk, bread, vegetables, all kinds of things. To keep track of how much was owed, they marked clay tablets. Marks morphed into shopping lists . . . math formulas . . . love letters . . . and magnificent stories!

Wow! Humans could write. They wrote down their stories about how I was born.

They moved and multiplied and celebrated life with colorful festivals. Spectacular cultures arose everywhere. Bustling cities appeared. Huge pyramids and temples reached into the sky. Astronomers studied the sun, moon and stars. Humans looked deeper and deeper into space.

Humans crossed boundaries everywhere. To enter the sea, they didn't wait to grow fins . . . they invented boats. To fly, they invented planes and space shuttles. They enveloped Earth with a World Wide Web. Humans crossed the boundary of time and took pictures that show how I looked when I was a baby Universe!

They saw that I *did* have a beginning . . . and that humans evolved inside of me!

Millions of Years Ago

65   60   55   50   45   40   35   30   25   20   15   10   5   Today

Dinosaur   Mammals   Rainforests   Whales   Rainforests   Grass   Apes   Hominids   Tools   Fire
Extinction   Spread   Everywhere   Shrink   Spreads

What wizards humans are!
But their cleverness has a dark side.

Humans became the most powerful Earthlings of all, but they forgot that they are made out of Earth's air, water and soil. They cut down trees and constructed buildings everywhere. They figured out how to power cars and planes by burning ancient fossil fuels. They made plastic and molded it into a zillion things. They used chemicals to grow more food. They acted as though everything belonged to them, to use as they wish.

Humans didn't realize they were poisoning Earth's lungs, veins and skin.

It became harder and harder for non-human Earthlings to live. They began to die. Then whole species went extinct, never to live again. Extinctions sped up. Yes, we've come to the part of the story that's happening right now. Every day, about another 50 Earthling species disappear forever. Even chimpanzees, your closest relatives, are in danger. I've told you about mass extinctions before. This time, human Earthlings are the major cause.

Earth is in the midst of the biggest mass extinction since the dinosaurs perished 65 million years ago.
What good can possibly come of this mess?

Millions of Years Ago

| 65 | 60 | 55 | 50 | 45 | 40 | 35 | 30 | 25 | 20 | 15 | 10 | 5 | Today |

Dinosaur Extinction   Mammals Spread   Rainforests Everywhere   Whales   Rainforests Shrink   Grass Spreads   Apes   Hominids   Tools Fire

In every crisis before, a surprising breakthrough happened.

Remember when I was less than a second old and nearly died during the Great Particle War? That's when tiny particles pulled together and turned into hydrogen.

And when your mother star exploded in a massive Supernova, remember what happened to her stardust? It fused into your Sun and planets.

And when bacteria nearly killed all life during the Oxygen Crisis, what happened? Enemy bacteria started cooperating like never before, without even knowing that their partnership would slowly morph into breathing plants and animals. They had exactly what it took to meet the crisis of their day.

Crises can unleash my cosmic creative powers. Today, my creative powers also live inside of *you*.

You may not know where you're headed. But you're part of something much bigger than humans and that's why you too have exactly the powers you need—the powers of imagination, love and decision making.

Yes, my dear humans, I'm relying on you to be heroes now! Working together with other Earthlings, you can turn this crisis into something magnificent—a new Earth—such as you've never seen before.

Dinosaur Mammals   Rainforests   Whales   Rainforests   Grass   Apes   Hominids   Tools Fire
Extinction Spread   Everywhere   Shrink   Spreads

Never forget that you are part of me. You are part of my wild and dazzling dream. Remember too, that I am inside you.

    *Every cell in your body is packed with hydrogen, made when I was born.

    *Your bones are hardened with calcium made by stars.

    *Your backbone was fashioned by fish.

    *The deepest part of your brain was built by reptiles.

    *The love you feel for another deepened inside the very first mammals.

    *Your awe-filled wonder began on starry nights around campfires, long, long ago.

My story lives inside of you and the story continues with you. Every day, you add more to the story. You are me being you, and through you I see myself . . . a huge restless Universe who loves to morph.

Our adventure has only just begun.
There's so much still to come.
Follow your dreams, my dear Earthlings.
They are my dreams too.

Love,

Your Universe

Millions of Years Ago

65 60 55 50 45 40 35 30 25 20 15 10 5 Today

Dinosaur Mammals   Rainforests   Whales   Rainforests   Grass   Apes   Hominids Tools Fire
Extinction Spread   Everywhere   Shrink   Spreads

P.S. Over the last 65 million years, I learned so many things . . . and mammals, especially you human mammals, had a lot to do with it.

I learned . . .

- how to make milk.

- that mice can evolve into horses and whales and humans.

- how to laugh, sing and cry.

- that communicating is one of my very favorite things to do.

- that I love to be lots of different things at the same time.

- that the older I get, the more complicated I am.

- that in a crisis, I evolve faster.

- that groups of Earthlings can do great things when they work together.

- how to love more deeply than ever before.

Yes, my dear Earthlings, I never stay the same for long. I'm always learning and morphing into things that never existed before. And you're part of my adventure!

Earth's Triumphs During the Age of Mammals

Earth's genetic language. There are over 20 million different species alive today and they're all related to each other because they evolved from a common ancestor. We all share a global genetic language called DNA (see glossary) that guides us in how to grow and behave. For example, humans share 80% of the same DNA with oak trees and 96% with chimpanzees, our closest relatives. Tiny changes in DNA, called mutations, lead to huge differences in body design and behavior. Slight variations create a mouse or a whale.

Out of reptiles . . . mammals and dinosaurs. Mammals and dinosaurs descended from reptiles. Mammals appeared around 200 million years ago. Like reptiles, monotreme mammals (such as the echidna and platypus) lay soft eggs. Two other groups of mammals give birth to live young: *marsupials and placental mammals*. Marsupials (like kangaroos) give birth to very tiny young that develop further in a pouch. Placental mammals (including humans) give birth to live young that are more developed.

Mammals are the only animals that make milk for their young. When mammals first began to evolve, their young licked sweat off their moms' hairy bellies. Over a long time, sweat transformed into fatty, sugary, nutritious milk.

Mammals, milk and mother love. Mammals have mammary glands that produce milk, and hair that keeps them warm—though some, such as whales, have lost their hair. Mammals, like birds, are warm blooded, which gives them a higher energy level and greater range of climate in which they can live. Unlike reptile young, who do not need parental care, mammal young are born helpless and depend on their mothers. A new kind of brain developed that helped mothers and their young bond with each other. Human love has its roots in this early relationship between mother and child. Many animals that aren't mammals also take care of their young in creative ways. Bird mothers and fathers work together to feed their young. Some squid mothers cradle their eggs in their tentacles, bathing the eggs in fresh seawater until they hatch. Caring for the next generation can take many forms.

Dinosaurs disappear and Earth goes mammal-crazy. When Earth's dinosaur adventure ended, mammals spread into new environments that shaped them into many different forms. So many species evolved during the Cenozoic that it is also known as the Age of Mammals.

Earth has a temperature. Over the last 65 million years, temperature changes have had a dramatic impact on life. Today, Earth's average temperature is 57 degrees Fahrenheit (14 degrees Celsius). That's a lot lower than the sweltering average temperature 50 million years ago of 82 degrees Fahrenheit (28 degrees Celsius).

Photograph by Andy Smith.

When dinosaurs perished, flowering plants, birds, insects and mammals spread and evolved into the spectacular diversity of species we see today. In this picture, a honey bee pollinates a crocus. Neither existed when dinosaurs roamed the earth.

At that time there were no ice caps and rainforests grew everywhere, even at the South Pole.

Flowering plants, birds, insects and mammals spread together. The first plants to evolve 500 million years ago, such as moss and later evergreens, reproduced through spores, not seeds. Flowering plants that produce seeds began to evolve before dinosaurs went extinct. And when dinosaurs perished, flowering plants took off, spreading everywhere along with birds, insects and mammals. Substantial evidence suggests that birds are descended from dinosaurs.

The energy feast. A cascade of energy starts with the sun. Photosynthesizing plants "eat" energy from the Sun and turn it into leaves, roots, and seeds that are consumed by plant-eating animals. Meat-eating animals consume the plant-eaters. When animals and plants die, bacteria eat (decompose) their bodies. Their molecules go back into the soil to be taken up through plant roots and transformed into life once again. This cycling pattern can be seen everywhere, even in

All marine mammals are descended from mammals that once walked on land. Killer whales, such as these, spend a lot of time in groups, socializing, and are very curious. They're coming up for a look around.

space. Stars are born out of the dust of other stars and when they die, their stardust, once again, forms into new stars.

Molecular versus fossil research. The story of whale research shows how different scientific disciplines can work together. Molecular research compares DNA from different species. Fossil research, by paleontologists, examines the physical remains (such as bones) of living things. For a long time, paleontologists believed that whales descended from the dog family. But molecular researchers disagreed. They reported that whales were genetically closer to hippos than to dogs. Then, in 2001, paleontologists discovered fossils in Pakistan that linked whales, porpoises and dolphins to hippos. That was a "Eureka!" moment in the world of research.

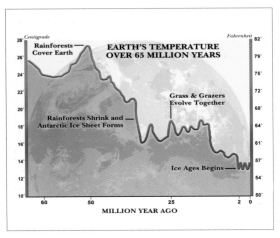

Even small changes in Earth's temperature cause life to evolve in dramatic ways. High temperatures brought rainforests. Lower temperatures brought grass and grazers who eat grass. Still lower temperatures brought ice ages and humans learned how to master fire.

Intelligence, communication and choice. Recent research reveals far greater intelligence and complex communication systems among animals than previously thought. Some even have their own form of democracy. When it's time to move from one location to another, individuals register their "vote" through sounds or body language. When species move into different environments, natural selection shapes them to fit the new place. As whale ancestors left land and pushed deeper into the sea, natural selection shaped their bodies for life under water. Decisions to move to a different environment can have a huge impact on evolution.

Earth cools down and new partnerships form. Symbiotic relationships propel evolution too. One example is the partnership between grazers and grass. As Earth cooled down about 25 million years ago, grass and grazers shaped each other in ways that helped both at the same time. Another such relationship developed between grazers and their intestinal bacteria. The bacteria digested food for their host, while helping themselves to dinner at the same time. (By the way, bacteria help you digest your food too.) We are imbedded in a web of symbiotic partnerships.

Living, learning, and loving in groups. Chimpanzees, our closest relatives, live in groups and by watching their elders, young chimps learn skills and social standards that enhance group living. Fair trade is one such behavior. They trade services and keep track of who performs favors, much as humans do. Friends groom one another, support each other in fights, and share food. The ability to remember who performs favors is not unique to primates. Research shows that bats and fish know upon whom they can rely, based on past experience. Emotions too, evolved long before chimpanzees, probably to enhance cooperation within groups. With good communication, individuals better fulfill their needs and work harder for the group. Bonding is particularly strong among those who have a long history of contributing to each other.

Cooperation within (and competition between) groups. Evolution rewarded those chimpanzee groups that cooperated within the group and successfully competed with other groups. Their genes were passed on. Chimpanzees are territorial, and neighboring groups establish boundaries between groups. Females and their young generally stay in the central area of the territory. Adolescent females move from one group to another, preventing too much inbreeding. Males patrol the perimeter and fiercely defend the boundary, killing strangers who venture inside. Chimpanzee research can reveal the roots of human aggression.

Apes stand up and humans begin to evolve. The dividing line between apes and hominids (early humans before the genus *Homo*) is the ability to stand up and walk for long periods. Apes can stand for awhile, but their bodies are structured for moving about on all fours. There are many theories about why some apes became bipeds. For females, walking on two legs may have made it easier to gather fruit and carry their young. Females may have selected males who brought them food, and males who could walk upright would have been the most able. Hominids did not evolve in a straight predictable line, and we do not know our direct ancestral line. At 7 million years old, *Sahelanthropus tchadensis*, with a chimp-sized brain, discovered in Chad in 2001, is the oldest known hominid.

Dogs and cats: from human foe to friend. About 40 million years ago, dogs and cats evolved in North America from a common ancestor, the weasel-like tree-climbing *Miacis*. Cats evolved first; later some cats evolved into dogs. How did humans begin their extraordinary friendship with dogs and cats, the dominant carnivores of Africa's savannah grasslands? We're not certain, but the relationship probably began to change when humans developed spears and javelins. As humans became better hunters, they may have even

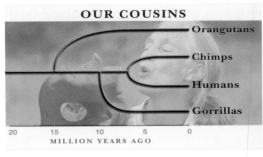

Chart by Adele Morgan

Humans and chimpanzees share a common ancestor who lived 5 to 8 million years ago. Chimpanzees are our closest relatives with 96% identical DNA. Pictured here is Jane Goodall, one the first researchers to study chimpanzee behavior, hooting with a chimpanzee cousin.

hunted collaboratively with dogs, much as they do even today. Over a long time, humans domesticated cats, dogs and many other animals.

Ice and fire. Two million years ago, Earth entered the time of Ice Ages, the coldest period during the Cenozoic Era. Over the last 750,000 years, glaciations have occurred roughly every 100,000 years. During glaciation peaks, glaciers covered 29% of Earth and in places were more than a mile thick. Between ice ages, Earth warmed up for about 12,000 years. It's been just about 12,000 years since the end of the last Ice Age. Could we be headed for another one? Ice ages forced humans to innovate. The earliest evidence of humans mastering fire dates back to 800,000 years ago in the Middle East. With that discovery, humans could live in colder climates. Cooking made food more digestible. Fire was a light source too. Fire may have increased group bonding and bonding between males and females. Fire probably played a crucial role in the development of human speech, imagination, and family life.

Lots of different humans? Does the great diversity of humans over the last 7 million years represent different species? There's so much diversity in humans today, yet we are all *Homo sapiens*. The line between human species has become much fuzzier with recent molecular research, leading scientists to wonder where one species leaves off and another begins. What is the relationship between *Homo sapiens* and Neanderthals? Did they interbreed? Neanderthals lived from about 150,000 to about 30,000 years ago. They inhabited a vast area roughly from England to Western Asia and south to the Red Sea. Recent evidence suggests they were far more intelligent than previously thought. They took care of the elderly, injured and infirm. They were skilled hunters and craftsmen who made tools and clothing, used fire, and buried their dead. They adjusted their diet through climate changes—hunting large game during ice age peaks and eating more fruits and vegetables in warmer climates. In short, Neanderthals were a lot like us.

Homo sapiens with a wild imagination. According to the Out of Africa Theory, *H. sapiens* emerged in Africa about 200,000 years ago. They reached the Near East by at least 90,000 years ago, Australia by 50,000 years ago, Europe by 40,000 years ago and the Americas by 13,000 years ago. Some scientists believe, however, that

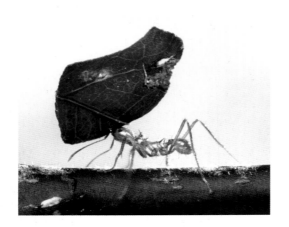

Humans weren't the first to develop agriculture. Fifty million years ago, leafcutter ants had already started fungus farms. They grew fungi on chewed leaves, fertilized with feces. They even had their own antibiotics to control harmful bacteria.

modern humans evolved from the interbreeding of many different kinds of humans.

Symbolic thought. Harsh ice age conditions may have brought about one of the most important *H. sapiens* innovations—symbolic thought. Expressed through jewelry, art, dress, and language, symbols increased group bonding, the ability to communicate complex thoughts, and gave a deeper purpose to life. Finely polished pointed awls made 70,000 years ago were discovered in South Africa. Jewelry began to appear about 30,000 years ago and may have been used as gifts to foster friendships, or to identify different groups. About 32,000 years ago, cave painters in France, using beautiful long-handled stone lamps to light their work, began creating remarkable cave paintings. Beauty was very important to H. sapiens. Symbolic thought evolved into myths, stories of creation, and spiritual beliefs. Female fertility figures sculpted beginning 25,000 years ago demonstrated an intense desire by H. sapiens to understand, connect with, and encourage the creative powers that bring forth life.

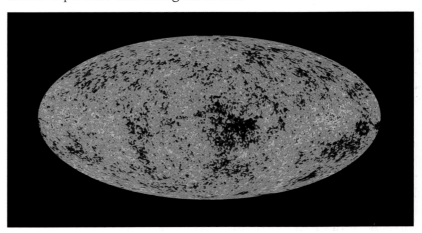

We're the first generation to have baby pictures of our Universe. This image, taken by the Wilkenson Microwave Anisotropy Probe (WMAP) is the first detailed full-sky map of the oldest light in the universe and shows how the universe looked when it was 380,000 years old. These globs of hydrogen clumped together, and over a long time ignited into stars. Everything we know came out of these globs of hydrogen. Long ago, humans intuited that the Universe had a beginning, and told creation stories the world over. Science now confirms that ancient intuition. (Photo courtesy of the NASA/WMAP Science Team.)

Agriculture. Coming out of the most recent Ice Age, about 12,000 years ago, humans discovered that seeds could grow into plants. It was a major breakthrough, enabling humans to settle down in large communities. Wheat and barley were cultivated in the Middle East; rice in Asia; and corn in the Americas. Dogs were domesticated and within a few thousand years, so were buffalo, pigs, chickens, cattle and horses. As for hot chocolate, the Mayans were the first to serve that, more than 2,600 years ago.

The rise of classical religions. As communities grew, the human spiritual quest became organized into classical religions. In China, the emphasis was on finding harmony with the rhythms of the universe. In India, the emphasis was on the impermanence of the visible world and on a transcendental realm beyond the mind. Religions with their roots in the

Middle East focused on an historical realism and the importance of the individual. Religious symbols and organizations helped people live together peaceably within their communities, but also caused conflict between communities.

The rise of science. Science shares with religion a quest for greater understanding, but does so in a different way – through observation and experimentation. The human scientific method has its roots in animal observation and experimentation. For example, crows in Japan have been observed placing nuts on the road, waiting patiently for cars to drive over them, then retrieving the cracked nuts. To perfect such a technique involved observation and experimentation. Early humans used science to develop better tools and spears and to control fire. Later they observed and recorded the seasons to grow more food. Over time, human science grew to include a complex quest to understand the beginning of the Universe and how it transformed into the Universe we know today.

The extinction crisis. Today, species are disappearing at a faster rate than at any other time since the dinosaurs perished 65 million years ago. Thirty two percent of amphibian species, 12 percent of birds, and 23 percent of mammals face extinction. Ten years ago there were 200,000 lions in Africa. Today, there are 20,000. Over 90% of large marine fish are gone. As species disappear, a domino effect accelerates as other species are impacted too. Over 25,000 species are disappearing every year, well over 50 per day. Natural and manmade causes include loss of habitat, invasive species, global warming, pollution, overexploitation, and disease. Even Earth's capacity to support life may be severely compromised.

A brain for today. When life began, there were no eyes or ears; and, there were no brains to interpret sight or sound. Brain evolution is a story of the interplay between environmental demands and inner capacities. Humans have a three-part brain developed over 500 million years. The **reptile** part of our brains—developed by fish and reptiles 450 to 300 million years ago—enables us to survive. With it, we can see, hear and smell. It guides us in sexual desire, the search for food and the fight or flight response when we're threatened. These behaviors are automatic and resist change. The early **mammal** brain (limbic system) includes instincts for parental care and enabled mammals to learn in more complex ways. The **neocortex** makes language, writing, and planning possible. It also enables humans to override short-term automatic responses of the reptile brain. Together, all three parts of the brain are much greater than the sum of the parts. How fascinating that our brains may have exactly the abilities needed for today—the drive to survive and the capacities to care and plan. Earth's current crisis may force us to evolve to yet another level of imagination and cooperation, the full magnitude of which we can't fully comprehend. Perhaps a newer and greater brain will join the brains we have today.

CREATING HUMANS
It took 13.7 billion years for the Universe to create humans.

THREE-PART BRAIN has reptile, early mammal, and late mammal parts.

EYES use light sensitive molecules, developed long before there were eyes.

THE BACKBONE was developed in fish 510 million years ago.

EMBRYONIC HUMANS recapitulate evolution of multicellular life on Earth.

WATER is made of hydrodgen (created inside the Big Bang) and oxygen (created inside stars). Sixty percent of human body weight is water.

WILD AND DAZZLING DREAMS are part of a Universe with a wild and dazzling imagination.

ROTATING SHOULDER was developed by primates in trees.

CELLS are directly descended from ancient single cell organisms.

DNA was developed in bacteria, the very first form of life.

CALCIUM in bones was created inside the burning furnaces of stars.

MITOCHONDRIA breathe oxygen inside every single cell. Long before humans evolved, they lived freely in the sea.

Adapted from a diagram in Awakening Universe, Emerging Personhood: The Power of Contemplation in an Evolving Universe, by Mary Coelho.

A story for today. Our ancestors intuited long ago that the Universe had a beginning, and now that insight has been confirmed through recent scientific discoveries. In a spectacular epic of evolution, the Universe transformed itself into what we know today, and continues to transform itself. We can see that humans evolved inside a vast creative Universe that has a story, full of drama—one that deepens our sense of a profound mystery beyond anything we can see or comprehend. We play a unique part in that we can reflect back on ourselves and the Universe as a whole. With our new vision, we can see how intimately we are part of our own planet Earth, enabling us to judge the value of our activities by the extent to which they benefit the Earth community as a whole.

Glossary

Apes Tailless primates including chimpanzee, gorilla, gibbon and orangutan. A branch of the ape group evolved into humans. Many scientists classify humans as a fifth great ape.

Cenozoic Era The most recent geologic era starting with the extinction of dinosaurs 65 million years ago. Modern continents formed; mammals, birds and plants diversified.

Culture Animal behavior passed from one generation to the next through observation, imitation and practice. Human culture also includes beliefs, institutions and art.

DNA (deoxyribonucleic acid) Carries genetic information in cells and can reproduce itself.

Genus A group of species more closely related to each other than to species from another genus.

Hominids Bipedal primate mammals including the genus *Homo* and earlier human-like species. New definitions also include the African apes.

Homo erectus A taller species of humans with a larger brain, flatter face and smaller teeth, that appeared around 1.9 million years ago and is regarded as an ancestor of modern humans.

Homo habilis A species of humans that lived between 2.0 and 1.5 million years ago and considered to be the earliest hominid to make tools.

Homo neanderthalensis A group of humans who lived in Europe and Western Asia between 150,000 and 30,000 years ago. Researchers disagree about whether Neanderthals are a separate species from modern humans.

Homo sapiens A species of archaic and modern humans that includes the subspecies *Homo sapien neanderthalensis* (Neanderthals) and *Homo sapiens sapiens* (modern humans).

Humans Members of the genus *Homo*, e.g. *Homo habilis*, *Homo erectus*, *Homo sapiens*. Humanlike primates who lived before the genus *Homo* are called hominids.

Hydrogen The very first element created within the newly born Universe, hydrogen has one proton and one electron. It's a gas and makes up 90 percent of the number of atoms in the Universe. All other elements were formed out of hydrogen.

Mammals Warm-blooded vertebrate animals, including humans, that have hair and produce milk for their young

Marsupials Mammals such as kangaroos and opossums whose females have a pouch containing teats where the young are fed and carried.

Mesozoic Era The geologic era from 245 to 65 million years ago. Reptiles evolved into dinosaurs and mammals. Flowering plants evolved toward the end of the Mesozoic.

Monkeys Long-tailed, medium-sized primates, including macaques, baboons, capuchins, and tamarins.

Monotremes Egg-laying mammals, such as the platypus.

Paleontology The study of fossils: remnants or impressions of organisms from past geological ages.

Placental mammals Mammals whose females have a placenta: a vascular, membranous organ in the uterus through which the mother provides food and oxygen to the embryo. All mammals except monotremes and marsupials are placental.

Primates Mammals with refined development of the hands and feet, a shortened snout, and a large brain.

Religion An organizational structure and system of beliefs, values, and practices that often center around reverence for a supernatural power.

Reptiles Air breathing, cold-blooded, usually egg-laying vertebrates covered with scales or horny plates, such as snakes, lizards, crocodiles, turtles, and dinosaurs. Mammals evolved out of reptiles.

Science The observation, identification, description, experimental investigation, and theoretical explanation of the natural world.

Species The most basic taxonomic group, whose members can interbreed.

Speciation The formation of new species, usually by the division of a single species into two or more distinct ones that do not interbreed.

Spiritual Relating to an awareness of, and sense of connection with, the animating force of the Universe, and a recognition of a meaning to existence that transcends one's immediate circumstances.

Symbiosis Intimate, long-lasting physical partnership between two different species.

Taxonomy Classification of living things into seven levels. From largest to smallest they are: kingdom, phylum, class, order, family, genus, species. The scientific name combines a genus name with a species name. For example: for *Homo habilis*, *Homo* is the genus and *habilis* is the species.

Books for Children and Teachers

Guide to Mammals, A wild journey with these extraordinary beasts by Ben Morgan (2003). Great pictures and text show the incredible diversity of mammals.

Mammals, A Dorling Kindersley Book (1993). Covers many different kinds of mammals in simple language and fascinating photographs.

Our Family Tree, An Evolution Story by Lisa Westberg Peters, illustrated by Lauren Stringer (2003). For K-3, places human evolution inside the ancient story of life.

Life On Earth: The Story of Evolution by Steve Jenkins (2002). For ages 6 to 10, torn collage images tell the story of evolution.

The Kid's Book of Awesome Stuff by Charlene Brotman, illustrated by Jeila Gueramian 2004). Activities and stories aimed for children 8 to 11 years old (great for younger and older children too) that show how humans are connected to everything.

Walking With Prehistoric Beasts by Tim Haines (2001). Scenes from the last 65 million years told in the present tense. Also on video.

Books for Adults

A Walk Through Time, From Stardust to Us, The Evolution of Life on Earth by Sidney Liebes, Elisabet Sahtouris, and Brian Swimme (1998). A great presentation of the Earth story with stunning photographs.

Awakening Universe, Emerging Personhood: The Power of Contemplation in an Evolving Universe by Mary Coelho (2002). Masterfully shows the spiritual significance of contemporary science.

Cosmic Fire; Local Sparks by Carmel Higgens (2005). A compelling personal story, from childhood in a traditional Catholic family to adulthood and embracing the epic of evolution.

Deeper Than Darwin: The Prospects for Religion in the Age of Evolution by John F. Haught (2004). Haught, a theologian, does a masterful job of showing how science and religion enrich our understanding of life through layered explanations.

Echo of the Big Bang by Michael Lemonick (2003). A fascinating story about a dedicated band of scientists and engineers behind WMAP, the Wilkensen Microwave Anisotropy Probe, which took pictures of the early universe.

Everybody's Story: Wising up to the Epic of Evolution by Loyal Rue (1999). Shows how the evolution of matter and consciousness can be a deep source of inspiration.

Evolution's Arrow, The Direction of Evolution and the Future of Humanity by John Stewart (2000). Argues that evolution is directional and progressive, producing organizations of greater scale and evolvability.

The Dream of the Earth by Thomas Berry (1988). A collection of important essays that discuss the primary role of Earth.

The Great Work by Thomas Berry (1999). Spells out the need to reorient our culture and institutions to Earth as a whole.

The Theory of Evolution:, A History of Controversy by Edward J. Larson (2001). A concise Study Guide and two very informative DVDs.

The Universe Story: From the Primordial Flaring Forth to the Ecozoic Era, A Celebration of the Unfolding of the Cosmos by Brian Swimme and Thomas Berry (1994). A classic that explores the inner and outer dimensions of evolution.

The Universe is a Green Dragon by Brian Swimme (2001). An eloquent discussion about the dynamics of the universe.

The MacMillan Illustrated Encyclopedia of Dinosaurs and Prehistoric Animals, A Visual Who's Who of Prehistoric Life by Dougal Dixon, Barry Cox, R.J. G. Savage, Brian Gardiner (1988). Great illustrations of mammal-like reptiles that evolved into mammals.

Videos

The Life of Mammals, Hosted by David Attenborough (2003). An epic story of the 4,000 mammal species in a breathtakingly beautiful, and humorous, journey.

The Powers of the Universe with Brian Swimme (2003). Shows the powers of the Universe that have been active since the beginning of time and are available to all.

The Unfolding Story (1993) An excellent introduction to the story of evolution, featuring many leaders in the field.

Other Resources

BBC website (www.bbc.co.uk/sn/prehistoric_life/human). Information about human evolution and reenactments of early human life.

Center for the Story of the Universe (www.brianswimme.org). Reflections, programs, books, and other materials by Brian Swimme.

The Great Story (www.thegreatstory.org). A website by Michael Dowd and Connie Barlow with a detailed timeline, articles, parables, and ritual celebrations for telling the story of the universe.

PBS website (www.pbs.org/evolution). Contains a wealth of information about Darwin and evolution.

Tree of Life Web Project (www.tolweb.org). Fantastic website that shows evolutionary history and characteristics of all groups of organisms.

Mary Ellen Hill (www.mehstories.com) is a professional storyteller in the San Francisco area whose specialty is "We Are The Stars That Sing: The Story of the Universe."

Jennifer Morgan, author of this book, tells stories for children and adults, provides teacher training, and leads adult workshops (www.UniverseStories.com).

Dear Reader,

Many have asked me, "Where's God in the story?"

The word "God" is purposefully not in the story so that it can be embraced by people of all religious traditions, or of none at all.

Another reason is that people usually refer to "God" as a transcendent, supernatural creator who exists outside the physical world.

Today, we're rediscovering a sense of divine creativity, not simply in the transcendent mode, but also as immanent, as present in the Universe itself.

My degree is in theology, not science. But I followed the advice of Thomas Berry, author of *The Dream of the Earth*, who advised Christians to study the primary scripture—the Universe itself. Accordingly for 8 years I lived and breathed science. I learned from some of the best scientists in the world in my hometown of Princeton, New Jersey. I also contemplated the 100-year old silver maple in my back yard. And I watched with wonder as my son matured into his teen years. I came to know—and to feel—a divinity immanent in the Universe that is far bigger and more mysterious than I had known before.

By reintegrating this immanent aspect of the Universe, the western world can reconnect to its own ancient traditions and to those of the wider community of people of all traditions.

Then we might ask, "Where is God *not* in the story?"

Jennifer Morgan
August 2006
Princeton, New Jersey

Jennifer Morgan's work as a storyteller, award winning author, educator and environmental advocate flows out of her love of the natural world and cosmology. Her storytelling evolved from bedtime stories for her son who wanted to know more and more, even the texture of the edge of the Universe. She believes that our cosmology stories fundamentally shape us—including our culture, religion, relationships, and self-concept. Ms. Morgan holds a degree in theology from the University of San Francisco. She studied cosmology, biology and anthropology at Princeton University. The first two books in this series received the highest review ratings from the American Association for the Advancement of Science (AAAS). Her first book, *Born With a Bang*, won Learning Magazine's Teachers Choice Award. Information about her programs and other books is available at www.UniverseStories.com.

Dana Lynne Andersen, M.A., is a multi media artist, writer and teacher with degrees in philosophy and consciousness studies. Her fine art seeks to reveal Being in the midst of Becoming, and to express the intelligence that swirls in energy and congeals into matter. She believes that as our "depth perception" expands outwardly (billions of galaxies have been discovered in our lifetime!) it is crucial to also expand inwardly. She is the founder of Awakening Arts Institute, nurturing a global network of artists through retreats, traveling workshops, exhibitions, and a small fine arts press. Workshop information and prints of the artwork in this book are available from www.awakeningarts.com.

Dawn Publications offers children's books that encourage an appreciation for the web of life on Earth.

ALSO BY JENNIFER MORGAN, ILLUSTRATED BY DANA LYNNE ANDERSEN

Born With a Bang: The Universe Tells Our Cosmic Story (Book One) The first in the Universe series tells the story of life from the very beginning to the creation of planet Earth. Winner of The Teacher's Choice Award.

From Lava to Life: The Universe Tells Our Earth Story (Book Two) Life begins to twitch and grow on a tumultuous planet, and survives numerous crises to become a dazzling array of bacteria . . . jellyfish . . . flowers . . . dinosaurs. Then the great meteor hits, dinosaurs are gone forever, but some life survives . . .

The Web at Dragonfly Pond, by Brian "Fox" Ellis, illustrated by Michael S. Maydak. Fishing with father becomes a life-long memory of how the web of life at the pond connects us all.

Eliza and the Dragonfly, by Susie Caldwell Rinehart, illustrated by Anisa Claire Hovemann. Almost despite herself, Eliza becomes entranced by the "awful" drag-onfly nymph—and before long, both of them are transformed.

A Tree in the Ancient Forest, by Carol Reed-Jones, illustrated by Christopher Canyon. The plants and animals around and under a grand old fir are remarkably connected to each other.

Girls Who Looked Under Rocks, by Jeannine Atkins. Six girls, from the 17th to the 20th century, didn't run from spiders or snakes but crouched down to take a closer look. They became pioneering naturalists, passionate scientists, and energetic writers or artists.

John Muir: My Life with Nature, by Joseph Cornell. John Muir's joyous enthusiasm for nature is contagious in this telling, mostly in his own words, of his remarkable adventures with nature.

Anthony Fredericks' award-winning series about place-based plant-and-animal communities, illustrated by Jennifer DiRubbio, includes: *Under One Rock: Bugs, Slugs and other Ughs; In One Tidepool: Crabs, Snails and Salty Tails; Around One Cactus: Owls, Bats and Leaping Rats; Near One Cattail: Turtles, Logs and Leaping Frogs;* and *On One Flower: Butterflies, Ticks and a few more Icks.*

Dawn Publications is dedicated to inspiring in children a deeper understanding and appreciation for all life on Earth. To review our titles or to order, please visit us at www.dawnpub.com, or call 800-545-7475.